DATE DUE

D1505814

Visual Geography Series®

NORTHERN IRELAND

...in Pictures

Prepared by
Geography Department

Lerner Publications Company
Minneapolis

Photo © Rachel Giese

A boy hugs his dog on a street in Londonderry, a major city in northwestern Northern Ireland.

This book is a newly commissioned title in the Visual Geography Series. The text is set in 10/12 Century Textbook.

LIBRARY OF CONGRESS CATALOGING-IN-PUBLICATION DATA

Northern Ireland in pictures / prepared by Geography Department, Lerner Publications Company.
    p. cm. – (Visual geography series)
    Includes index.
    Summary: Introduces the topography, history, society, economy, and governmental structure of Northern Ireland.
    ISBN 0-8225-1898-8 (lib. bdg.)
    1. Northern Ireland–Juvenile literature. [1. Northern Ireland.] I. Lerner Publications Company. Geography Dept. II. Series: Visual geography series (Minneapolis, Minn.).
DA990.U46N666 1991
941.6–dc20   90-24151

International Standard Book Number: 0-8225-1898-8
Library of Congress Card Catalog Number: 90-24151

VISUAL GEOGRAPHY SERIES®

Publisher
Harry Jonas Lerner
Associate Publisher
Nancy M. Campbell
Senior Editor
Mary M. Rodgers
Editors
Gretchen Bratvold
Dan Filbin
Tom Streissguth
Photo Researcher
Kerstin Coyle
Editorial/Photo Assistants
Marybeth Campbell
Colleen Sexton
Consultants/Contributors
Christabel D. Grant
Sandra K. Davis
Designer
Jim Simondet
Cartographer
Carol F. Barrett
Indexers
Kristine S. Schubert
Sylvia Timian
Production Manager
Gary J. Hansen

Photo © Rachel Giese

In a suburb of Belfast, the capital city of Northern Ireland, an arch is decorated with British flags and pictures of the British royal family.

Acknowledgments

Title page photo © 1991 Barbara Beirne.

Elevation contours adapted from *The Times Atlas of the World*, seventh comprehensive edition (New York: Times Books, 1985).

2 3 4 5 6 7 8 9 10 – JR – 06 05 04 03 02 01 00 99 98 97

Bagpipers in Blackwatertown, a city in the southern part of the country, perform during festivities on a Roman Catholic holiday. Throughout Northern Ireland, religious and political groups use parades and other public celebrations to express their beliefs.

Contents

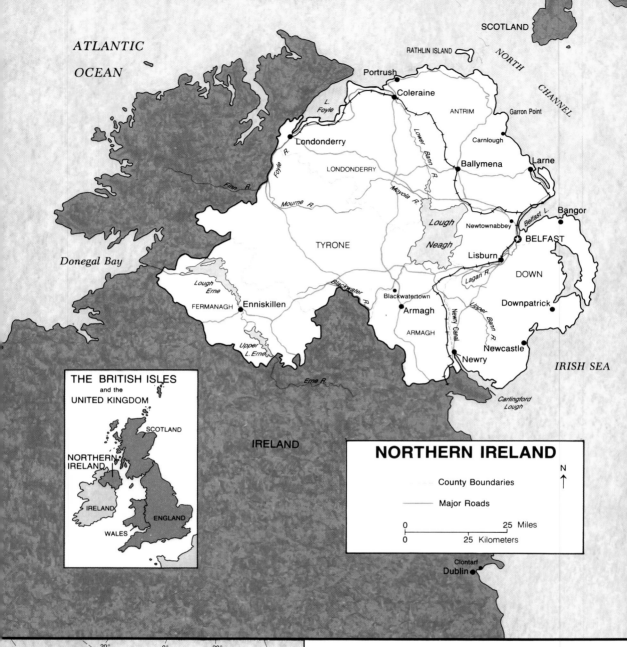

ATLANTIC

OCEAN

SCOTLAND

RATHLIN ISLAND

NORTH

CHANNEL

Portrush

Coleraine

ANTRIM

Garron Point

L.
Foyle

Carnlough

Londonderry

LONDONDERRY

Ballymena

Larne

Donegal Bay

Foyle R.

Finn R.

Mourne R.

Lower Bann R.

Moyola R.

Lough

Neagh

Newtownabbey

Belfast L.

Bangor

BELFAST

TYRONE

Lisburn

Lagan R.

DOWN

Lough
Erne

FERMANAGH

Enniskillen

Blackwater R.

Blackwatertown

Armagh

ARMAGH

Newry Canal

Upper Bann R.

Downpatrick

Newcastle

Upper
L. Erne

Newry

IRISH SEA

Erne R.

Carlingford
Lough

IRELAND

NORTHERN IRELAND

N
↑

——— County Boundaries

——— Major Roads

| 0 | | | | 25 | Miles |
| 0 | | | 25 | | Kilometers |

Clontarf
Dublin

THE BRITISH ISLES
and the
UNITED KINGDOM

SCOTLAND

NORTHERN
IRELAND

IRELAND

ENGLAND

WALES

60°

20°

0°

20°

Arctic

Circle

NORWEGIAN

SEA

EUROPE
NORTHERN
IRELAND

| 0 | | 400 | Miles |
| 0 | | 400 | Kilometers |

60°

NORTH
ATLANTIC
OCEAN

20°

40°

40°

MEDITERRANEAN SEA

0°

METRIC CONVERSION CHART
To Find Approximate Equivalents

WHEN YOU KNOW:	MULTIPLY BY:	TO FIND:
AREA		
acres	0.41	hectares
square miles	2.59	square kilometers
CAPACITY		
gallons	3.79	liters
LENGTH		
feet	30.48	centimeters
yards	0.91	meters
miles	1.61	kilometers
MASS (weight)		
pounds	0.45	kilograms
tons	0.91	metric tons
VOLUME		
cubic yards	0.77	cubic meters
TEMPERATURE		
degrees Fahrenheit	0.56 (*after* subtracting 32)	degrees Celsius

A trio of young Northern Irish girls practices on traditional instruments in their classroom. Music is an important element of education as well as Irish culture. From an early age, students learn the songs that belong to specific religious and political groups with which their families have ties.

Introduction

Northern Ireland is the smallest country within the European nation called the United Kingdom of Great Britain and Northern Ireland. Part of the British Isles —a group of islands in northwestern Europe—Northern Ireland shares the island of Ireland with the independent Republic of Ireland. Also within the United Kingdom are England, Wales, and Scotland. Those three countries are located on the island of Great Britain.

Northern Ireland and the Republic of Ireland not only occupy the same island, they also share a long and troubled history. Invaded several times during the last 2,000 years, portions of the island of Ireland were conquered or inhabited by Celtic, Viking, Norman, and English groups.

In the twentieth century, the relationship between the people on the island of Ireland to those on Great Britain has generally been difficult. The majority of the people in Northern Ireland have maintained close ties with Britain. These Northern Irish are called Unionists because they want to continue their country's union with the rest of the United Kingdom.

In contrast, most of the people in the Republic of Ireland and a large minority in Northern Ireland favor making the entire island a single, independent nation. These people are known as Nationalists. This deep difference in viewpoint between Nationalists and Unionists has frequently caused violence in Northern Ireland.

In spite of these troubles, Northern Ireland has a diverse economy. With plentiful rains and lush grasslands, most of Northern Ireland is suited to farming. But, unlike the rest of the island, this country also has a long-established manufacturing region. The traditional industries of linen making and shipbuilding are located on the northeastern coast, mainly around the capital city of Belfast.

As part of the United Kingdom, Northern Ireland belongs to the European Union (EU)—an economic association of western European nations. Foreign funds and money from the United Kingdom are helping Northern Ireland to develop more industries. This move may overcome the country's high unemployment rate. The United Kingdom also gives considerable financial aid to Northern Ireland to end inequalities that years of political strife have caused.

Lush, level farmland in County Antrim is typical of the terrain in this eastern section of Northern Ireland.

Business is brisk in metropolitan neighborhoods in Northern Ireland. The United Kingdom, of which Northern Ireland has been a part since 1920, has funded the growth of Northern Irish commercial and industrial areas.

Giant's Causeway along the Antrim coast is a series of rock columns that were formed by volcanic activity millions of years ago. The six-sided columns are so precisely made that legends have evolved to explain their shape. One of the tales suggests that an Irish giant arranged the stones to build a path for crossing the North Channel to Scotland.

1) The Land

Northern Ireland occupies about one-sixth of Ireland, the second largest island in the British Isles. These islands are clustered in the Atlantic Ocean at the northwestern corner of mainland Europe. The Atlantic borders Northern Ireland to the north. To the west and south, along a 303-mile boundary, is the Republic of Ireland. Northern Ireland's southeastern coast faces the Irish Sea. Scotland, another country in the United Kingdom, sits only 13 miles to the east of Northern Ireland across the North Channel. At its widest point, Northern Ireland is 110 miles across, and its length from north to south is 85 miles. The country has 330 miles of shoreline.

In most places, the seas around the British Isles are shallow. The waters that lie near Northern Ireland's coast are only about 300 feet deep and provide good commercial and sport fishing.

Northern Ireland consists of six of the original nine counties of a centuries-old Irish province known as Ulster. The six counties are Armagh, Fermanagh, Tyrone, Londonderry, Antrim, and Down. With an area of 5,452 square miles, Northern Ireland is about the size of the state of Connecticut.

Topography

Northern Ireland contains a series of low mountains with relatively steep valleys. A region of fertile lowlands lies approximately in the middle of the country. Most of the farmable land is used as pasture for livestock and for growing crops on small farms.

In the center of Northern Ireland sits Lough Neagh, the largest lake in the British Isles. (*Lough* means "lake" or "bay" in Gaelic, the ancient language of the island.)

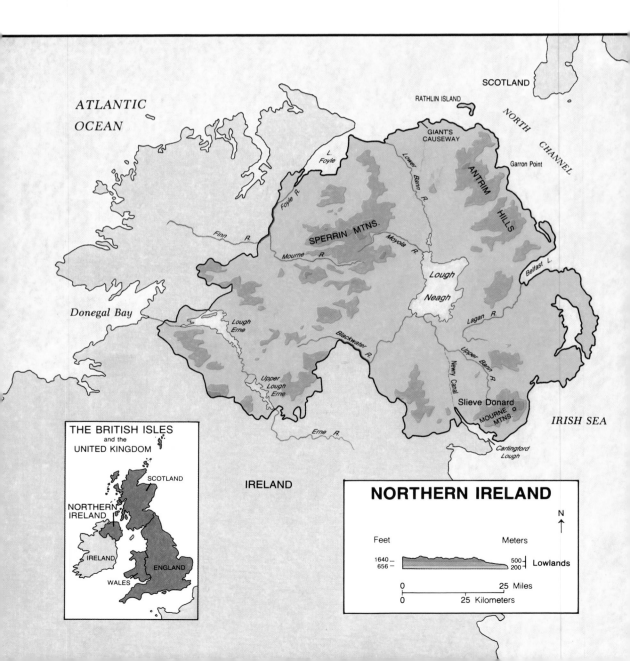

The pounding waves of the Irish Sea have uncovered layers of red sandstone and evidence of ancient lava flows in Northern Ireland's jagged shore.

Sheep graze on gently rolling pastureland that surrounds the Sperrin Mountains on the western side of Northern Ireland.

The Mourne Mountains are among Northern Ireland's rockiest landforms. Farmers remove large stones from the region's foothills, using the rocks to mark off boundaries and to make barriers for grazing animals.

Located six miles off Northern Ireland's coast, Rathlin Island has many limestone cliffs. Strong waves have eroded the shore, creating pointed pillars and rugged crags.

The 153-square-mile lake is shallow, and people use it for fishing and recreational activities.

In the northwestern counties of Londonderry and Tyrone, the Sperrin Mountains rise to a height of just over 2,000 feet above sea level. The rounded tops of the Sperrin range form gently sloping peaks. The taller Mourne Mountains on the southeastern coast of the country are jagged. This range contains Northern Ireland's highest mountain, Slieve Donard (2,796 feet). (*Slieve* means "mountain" in Gaelic.) The Antrim Hills on the country's northeastern coast rise between 1,000 and 1,500 feet in height.

Many parts of Northern Ireland's coastline are marked by cliffs that drop sharply into the sea. The jagged faces of some cliffs reveal underlying granite rock, and others are made of chalk. Giant's Causeway, an unusual formation of about 40,000 six-sided columns, lies on the country's northern coast. Quick-cooling lava that flowed about 70 million years ago produced the thousands of rock pillars.

Rivers and Lakes

Northern Ireland has many rivers. The Upper Bann River starts in the Mourne Mountains and flows northwestward for 25 miles before entering Lough Neagh. The waterway exits the lake as the Lower Bann River and follows a 33-mile course to the North Channel.

The 72-mile-long Erne River begins in the Republic of Ireland and crosses the border into Northern Ireland as it flows northward. The stream then broadens to form two lakes—Upper Lough Erne and Lower Lough Erne. The river leaves the lakes and feeds into Donegal Bay on the northern coast.

Courtesy of Northern Ireland Tourist Board

In the southern part of Northern Ireland, a fisherman tries his skill in Upper Lough Erne, where sport fishing is a popular activity for residents and visitors.

Photo © Rachel Giese

Rental boats line one of the harbors near Enniskillen, a town that lies midway between the upper and lower sections of Lough Erne.

A rope bridge suspended 80 feet above the sea connects the mainland of Northern Ireland to Carrick-a-Rede, a small island that is only 60 feet off the northern coast. The bridge is a popular – if daring – stop for tourists.

The short Finn and Mourne rivers join to form the Foyle River in the northern part of the country. The Foyle passes through the city of Londonderry, and as the river empties into the Atlantic Ocean it widens into an estuary (or bay) called Lough Foyle. The Foyle River also marks Northern Ireland's northwestern boundary with the Republic of Ireland.

The Lagan River enters Belfast Lough on the North Channel. Engineers have expanded the small stream of Newry into a canal that flows southward into Carlingford Lough. The Foyle, Belfast, and Carlingford loughs provide good harbors for sea vessels traveling to and from Northern Ireland.

Climate

Northern Ireland's average temperatures range from 40° F in January, the coldest month, to about 58° F in July, the warmest month. Winds that reach the country from the Atlantic Ocean help to make summers cool and winters mild. Most of the time, ocean breezes come from the west. In summer, the ocean cools the warm winds heading toward the island, bringing cooler temperatures. In winter, the sea heats the cold winds that pass over it. As a result, the warmed air currents raise winter temperatures on the island.

Winds from the Atlantic also carry plenty of rainfall, which is fairly evenly distributed throughout the year. In the northern

In the highland areas of County Antrim, sheep graze on snow-dusted slopes. Most of Northern Ireland's precipitation comes as rain, which falls throughout the year.

Photo © Rachel Giese

Primroses, which bloom in the spring, thrive in the moist soil of Northern Ireland.

A hunter prepares to release weasel-like ferrets that will help him flush out small game, especially rabbits. Ferrets have long, slim bodies, and when frightened, they give off a strong odor.

part of the country, about 40 inches of rain fall annually. The southern part of the country typically receives about 30 inches of precipitation.

With wet conditions persisting over hundreds of years, soggy areas called peat bogs have developed in parts of Northern Ireland. The bogs contain layers of vegetation that have only partly decayed in the moist earth. The layers build up over time, making a thick crust of turf that is known as peat. When cut into blocks and dried, this material can be burned as fuel.

Flora and Fauna

Until about 7,000 years ago, a land bridge linked the island of Ireland to Europe. Rising ocean levels then separated Ireland and the other British Isles from the continent. Once isolated, Ireland's animals and plants became much less diverse than those in Europe. In addition, human settlement and farming patterns altered or destroyed the natural habitats of many of the island's native species.

Northern Ireland hosts many of the same animals and plants that exist throughout the rest of the island of Ireland. A wide selection of ferns and rushes (hollow-stemmed plants) covers marshy regions. Forested areas extend over less than 5 percent of the country, but small, thick stands of oak, birch, ash, hazel, alder, and willow dot the countryside. The Northern Irish government has begun a reforestation program. Gardeners raise a variety of plants. One kind—a type of orchid named *Spiranthes stricta*—is distinctive to the Upper and Lower Bann river valleys.

In some parts of the island, scientists have found the remains of now-extinct animals—such as giant Irish deer, arctic foxes, and arctic lemmings (rodents that turn white in the winter). A few of these skeletons are about 40,000 years old. In the present era, foxes, badgers, otters, ferrets, and Irish hares are abundant, and freshwater sponges (a type of sea animal)

Courtesy of Northern Ireland Tourist Board

Constructed in the 1800s, Belfast Castle is modeled after the style of seventeenth-century Scottish mansions. The building is a landmark of Belfast, the capital and largest city in Northern Ireland.

inhabit Ireland's lakes. Made of interconnected fibers that form the animals' skeletons, these sponge species exist nowhere else in Europe. A whitefish called the pollan lives in Lough Neagh and in Upper and Lower Lough Erne.

Natural Resources

Northern Ireland has few natural resources. The country contains significant deposits of basalt rock, peat, limestone, and granite. These raw materials provide the country with some fuel and construction materials. Chalk, sand, and gravel are also used in the building trades.

Although other parts of the British Isles have large coal deposits, very little coal is mined in Northern Ireland. Most raw materials for creating energy must be imported from other parts of the United Kingdom. Shipments of coal, oil, and natural gas arrive regularly in Northern Ireland's ports.

Cities

Belfast (population 300,000) is Northern Ireland's capital city. It lies on the country's eastern coast at the mouth of the Lagan River, which flows into a bay named Belfast Lough. Nearness to the sea makes Belfast a good port and has allowed the city to develop a large shipbuilding industry. Workers construct ocean liners and naval vessels in Belfast's huge dry dock. This facility, the largest in the world, lifts boats completely out of the water for cleaning and repair. Belfast is also known for linen making, food processing, and aircraft construction.

The name Belfast comes from the Gaelic words *Beal Feirste,* which mean "mouth of the Farset," a stream that joins the Lagan. Hills and many ancient castles surround the city. Because of frequent violence within Belfast, the government has banned private cars in the center of the city. This limitation has created an attractive and popular walking area in the oldest part of

15

Londonderry nestles alongside the Foyle River in the northwestern corner of the country.

Flying the British flag, Belfast's city hall also carries a political banner that rejects closer ties with the Republic of Ireland, which lies to the south.

Northern Ireland's commercial, cultural, and political hub.

Londonderry (population 97,000) rises along the banks of the Foyle River on the northern coast of the country. Called Derry by many of its residents, the city took this part of its name from the Gaelic word *doire,* which means "oak grove." By the 1700s, Londonderry's inhabitants had built a thick wall with several gates around the city for protection and defense. In the twentieth century, townspeople and tourists walk on top of this wall through Londonderry's older sections. These areas contain long brick buildings that were once linen-making factories—the major industry in Londonderry at one time.

Londonderry shows the effects of the violence that has long troubled Northern Ireland. Catholics and Protestants have often clashed along the borders of Bogside, a largely Catholic neighborhood. People from Bogside have put up barricades to keep out the Protestant police force. In this part of Londonderry, as in many other sections of the city, some buildings have been partly destroyed by fires, bombings, and gunfire.

In the Belfast suburb of Lisburn, workers survey bomb damage to several shops. The Irish Republican Army (IRA), an Irish Catholic military group, set off the explosion as a way of expressing its hatred for the Protestant-dominated government of Northern Ireland.

About 30 miles north of Belfast lies the seaside town of Carnlough. Known as a center for limestone quarrying, Carnlough is also a hub of summertime sport fishing.

In Northern Ireland, Armagh is the headquarters of both the Roman Catholic Church and the Protestant Church of Ireland. Within the city, each of these religious sects has a cathedral named after Saint Patrick. This fifth-century missionary brought the Christian faith to the Celtic inhabitants of the island.

Armagh (population 14,500) lies in the southern part of Northern Ireland. This historic city traces its roots back to the sixth century, when a missionary named Patrick brought Christianity to the Irish people. In the 1900s, Armagh became the administrative center for both the Catholic and Protestant churches. The city is also known for the study of astronomy. Armagh's first observatory dates from 1789.

The eighteenth-century observatory in Armagh was designed to map the stars using the most updated equipment of the period. The observatory now includes video and computer shows to educate visitors.

A reconstructed watchtower overlooks the surrounding countryside in a park in the center of Northern Ireland. The watchtower's function—to allow residents to see approaching enemies—is a reminder of how often the region has been attacked in its long history.

2) History and Government

Archaeologists have learned a lot about the first inhabitants of Ireland by unearthing jewelry, utensils, pottery, and weapons from burial chambers. These finds have led historians to think that people were living on the island by at least 3000 B.C. The early Irish made tombs of stone and built gathering areas next to them. Archaeologists have also dug up earthen burial mounds that the ancient residents built on hilltops.

Among the objects in the tombs was beaker pottery—large earthenware containers that are similar to other artifacts found in Britain and on the continent of Europe. The presence of these objects in Ireland shows that people traveled back and forth between the British Isles and the European mainland.

The weapons in the burial mounds indicate that the early Irish hunted animals and caught fish. By 2000 B.C., the Irish had become farmers and were relying less on hunting. They also had begun to fashion objects from gold, copper, and bronze. Archaeologists have discovered pieces of metalwork from Ireland in mainland Europe, and these finds suggest that trade occurred between the two regions.

The Celts

By 250 B.C., groups of Celtic people from north central Europe had sailed to Ireland. The Celts had also spread into France, Spain, Greece, and the other British Isles.

A warlike people, the Celts took great pride in their military conquests. They decorated their weapons, jewelry, dwellings, and tombs with intricate curves and spirals. The Celts had a lasting impact on the British Isles, spreading their language, arts, and customs throughout England, Wales, Scotland, and Ireland.

The Irish Celts lived in small groups headed by a chief. These small kingdoms were called *tuatha* and were made up of people who had a common ancestor. Within each tuatha, families formed subgroups that had specific functions. One set of families ruled, for example. Another

Photo © Rachel Giese

The Ardboe cross stands 18 feet tall on the shores of Lough Neagh. Built in the tenth century, the cross is decorated with scenes from the Bible.

Independent Picture Service

This granite statue of Saint Patrick commemorates the 1500th anniversary of the missionary's landing at Armagh. "Saint Patrick" is written in the Gaelic language at the base of the memorial. Gaelic, an ancient Celtic tongue, is still spoken by many people in Northern Ireland.

In the ninth century, Viking raiders from Norway and Denmark invaded the island of Ireland in wooden warships. Designed to sail swiftly up rivers, these boats allowed the Vikings to launch surprise attacks against Celtic people and Catholic religious buildings. The raiders robbed Armagh on several occasions.

Photo by Irish Tourist Board, Dublin

subgroup consisted of farmers and workers. The Celtic tuatha also included poets, legal advisers (called *brehon*), and scholarly priests (known as Druids). For the most part, the tuatha were fiercely independent of each other. Only under the influence of a particularly strong chief did one tuatha combine with another.

In the fourth century A.D., a few chiefs gained power over other tuatha. Through conquests and alliances, these powerful chiefs established five major territories in Ireland, namely Connacht, Munster, Leinster, Meath, and Ulster. These territories are known as the "five-fifths" of Ireland. Ulster included the area that is presently called Northern Ireland.

In the late fourth century, more than 100 tuatha were competing for power. Niall of the Nine Hostages, whose name boasted of his hostage-taking skills, was the first chief to control most of the island of Ireland. Two of his sons, Eogan and Conall, focused their power in Ulster, and their families maintained authority there for several centuries.

Patrick at Armagh

Some of the chiefs of Ireland made raids on Great Britain and on the European mainland, taking riches and capturing hostages for ransom. Among the captives of one raid was a 16-year-old boy who would later be known as Saint Patrick. Sold as a slave in about A.D. 405, Patrick herded animals in northeastern Ireland for several years. He escaped to Europe in 411 and eventually became a Christian priest and missionary.

21

In 432 Patrick returned to the northern part of Ireland and began his missionary work. The center of his activity was Armagh in northeastern Ireland, where he and other missionaries built a church and taught the Latin language to many of their Christian converts. Monasteries (religious communities of men or women) developed in Ireland during Patrick's era and became centers of worship in the tuatha. These communities also set up schools that eventually attracted students from many parts of Europe.

From Patrick's time onward, Christian traditions greatly influenced Irish culture. The impact of Irish Christianity also extended to Great Britain and to the rest of Europe. Monks who left Ireland as missionaries set up schools that became well-known centers of scholarly and religious learning.

During the sixth century, the work of the monks and their schools fostered the beginnings of Gaelic literature, music, and local arts. Some of the period's most beautiful artworks involved calligraphy (ornate hand-lettering). Monks copied religious texts and decorated them with intricate designs and vibrant colors. Among the most famous manuscripts written in this fashion was the Book of Kells, a copy of the Christian Gospels made in about the eighth century.

Viking Attacks

At the end of the eighth century, raiders from Norway and Denmark invaded Ireland by sea. Known as Vikings, these people arrived in long, swift boats that were able to travel along rivers to the island's interior. The Vikings attacked monasteries and looted many Christian churches, including those at Armagh.

The Vikings killed many Irish people and took precious gold and silver church objects as treasure. The attackers also destroyed some of the finely illustrated religious texts, hoping to dislodge Chris-

Photo © Rachel Giese

This plaque on the side of a church in Armagh marks the burial spot of Brian Boru—the eleventh-century Irish king who defeated the Vikings. The hero's last name is written on the plaque according to an ancient Gaelic spelling.

tianity and to replace it with their own beliefs. The Vikings were most successful in conquering territory in the southern parts of the island. The inhabitants of the northern region put up stronger resistance. Even so, the Viking invaders also established outposts in the north.

By the mid-ninth century, Irish chiefs began to repel some of the Viking attacks. As the tuatha joined together for defense, they won more victories. By the eleventh century, they had united under a leader named Brian Boru and had made him king of all Ireland. The Irish fought a decisive battle against the Vikings at Clontarf, on the eastern coast, in 1014. Boru's forces defeated the Vikings, but Boru was killed in the battle.

The victory at the Battle of Clontarf ended the Viking invasions, but not all Vikings returned to their homelands. Many remained in Ireland and were absorbed over time into the Irish population. The Vikings contributed to Irish life and culture by developing trade and by establishing new market towns.

The Normans Invade Ireland

For about 150 years, the Irish experienced no significant invasions. But in 1066 the

Normans from France conquered the English throne. This event led to another period of conquest in Ireland. By 1167 the first Norman soldiers had set foot on the island at the invitation of Dermot Mac-Murrough, an Irish chief who had lost his land. He urged the Normans to take over Ireland so that he could win back his own property. Using armor, mounted soldiers, and archers with longbows, the Normans attacked the Irish forces.

At first the Irish army was able to stop the Normans and to control MacMurrough. But this unified Irish force could not compete against the better weapons and strategies of the Normans. Even though the Irish troops resisted fiercely, the Norman forces usually outnumbered them and defeated the islanders again and again.

In 1177 a Norman named John de Courcy took his army north into Ulster and overcame the region's Irish chief. Although de Courcy claimed much territory, he was not able to move beyond the Upper and Lower Bann rivers. In keeping with Norman practice, de Courcy built castles in the conquered territory to strengthen his claims to the land. Norman strongholds dominated the towns of Coleraine, Downpatrick, and Newry, and de Courcy ruled this region until he died in 1219.

The Irish Fight Back

By the mid-1200s, the Normans had established walled towns in many parts of Ireland. Irish chiefs in the north and west were more successful than leaders in other areas at keeping territories out of Norman hands. As a way to strengthen royal power, the Norman kings of England introduced a system of landownership called feudalism. This system gave the king ultimate authority over all royal lands. The monarch then allowed nobles to use the land in return for their loyalty and for a share of the land's earnings. The nobles, in turn, made similar arrangements with the farmers who worked these royal holdings.

The Norman kings also introduced their laws and style of governing to Ireland. They divided the territory into counties, each of which had a local council and officials. By the end of the thirteenth century, a parliament began meeting regularly to set taxes and to make laws. At this same time in England, the distinction between Normans and English began to blur as intermarriage produced a mixed Norman-English population.

The Irish remained a distinct group, however, and their chiefs tried to take back their homeland. To help them in their fight, the Irish hired skilled warriors from Scotland. Norman nobles who were long-time residents of Ireland also aided the Irish to free themselves from the limits imposed by the Norman-English kings.

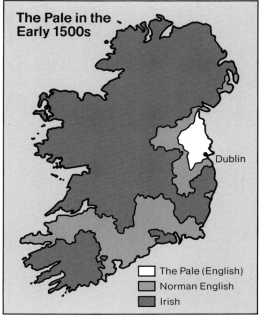

The Pale in the Early 1500s

Dublin

The Pale (English)
Norman English
Irish

Artwork by Laura Westlund

In the 1300s and 1400s, the territory of the Pale—the area of English control in Ireland—centered around Dublin. The northeastern part of the island, which would one day become Northern Ireland, remained independent until the early sixteenth century.

Anti-Irish Laws

As the Irish armies gained strength, the Norman-English rulers responded by passing new laws that made it a crime for the Normans to associate with the Irish. Despite these measures, the Irish chiefs and their Norman allies continued to fight the Norman-English rulers during the 1300s and 1400s. As decades passed, the efforts of the islanders succeeded. The area of Norman-English authority—known as the Pale—was reduced to territory on the east central coast of Ireland. Northeastern Ireland became nearly independent.

In the late 1400s, the English king Henry VII began making stricter Irish laws in Ireland to keep the Irish from regaining power. He appointed an administrator named Edward Poynings to rid Ireland of its deep traditions and to weaken the Irish identity. To carry out these orders, Poynings directed the Irish Parliament to restrict the civil rights of the Irish people. For example, they could no longer gather freely or speak openly against the government. Opposition to these laws among the islanders was fierce, and soon the king removed Poynings from office.

Ulster and the Reformation

Henry VIII became king of England in 1509. In 1534 he established himself as the leader of a new church in England and tried to impose a different Christian religion—Protestantism—on Ireland. King Henry's attempts to break Ireland's centuries-old ties with the Roman Catholic form of Christianity met strong resistance.

The king offered to increase the landholdings of Irish nobles who would recognize him as head of the new church. Few of the Irish, and none of those in Ulster, accepted the king's proposal. In 1541 Henry

Photo by Mansell Collection

In the 1530s, the English king Henry VIII *(seated center)* named himself head of the new Protestant religion in England. The Irish, who were mainly Roman Catholic, remained faithful to the Catholic church. In 1541 the English Parliament proclaimed Henry VIII king of Ireland. He tried to get Irish nobles to accept Protestantism by offering them land and titles of nobility. Few Irish became Protestants during Henry's reign.

Conscientia mille

Photo by Bettmann/Hulton

By kneeling and swearing an oath, Hugh O'Neill of Tyrone pretended to submit to the representative of England's Queen Elizabeth. Soon afterward O'Neill launched a successful attack against her forces. Following this early victory, O'Neill and his army were defeated at the Battle of Kinsale in 1601.

took the title of king of Ireland to gain political and religious support. But most Irish leaders refused to recognize the English monarch's authority and tried to maintain their independence.

English Protestants looted many Roman Catholic churches during the introduction of Protestantism. Henry VIII outlawed monasteries, and a number of them were burned down. Roman Catholicism, however, remained strong throughout the island, despite continuing religious oppression. Only a small percentage of Irish people supported the new faith.

In 1547 Henry's son and successor—Edward VI—made Protestantism the official religion of Ireland. Edward's troops acted vigorously to apply this law, arresting nobles who refused to become Protestants and seizing their property.

Edward gave much of this land to English Protestants who had immigrated to Ireland. They participated in the plantation system, whereby the new arrivals were "planted" on Irish soil. These transfers of land from the Irish to people sponsored by

the king of England continued under Edward's successors—Mary I and, later, Elizabeth I. The Irish resisted seizures of property throughout Ireland but nowhere more strongly and successfully than in Ulster.

ELIZABETH I AND HUGH O'NEILL

Elizabeth I became ruler of England in 1558. The Irish Parliament—which was under English control—named Elizabeth head of the Irish church in 1560. English, rather than Gaelic, became the language used in religious services. The Irish people continued to fight England's attempts to impose the Protestant religion on them and to prohibit the use of Gaelic.

Hugh O'Neill of Tyrone—an Irish leader from Ulster—attacked Elizabeth's troops in 1594 and defeated them at Armagh. To put down the Irish rebellion, a large English force arrived in 1599. O'Neill asked for help from the leaders of Spain, who were rivals of the English monarch. When a small Spanish fleet came to Ireland, its commander insisted on mounting a surprise

25

Courtesy of James H. Marrinan

An Irish coin *(top)* carries a likeness of the Catholic king of England James II who tried to reestablish good relations with Ireland. His Protestant son-in-law and daughter, William of Orange and Mary *(bottom),* overthrew James in 1690. Protestants from northern Ireland fought alongside William and Mary's troops.

attack. The raid ended badly for the Irish when the English defeated the Irish and Spanish forces at the Battle of Kinsale in 1601.

To prevent other revolts from breaking out in Ireland, the English took away all remaining Irish legal and religious rights. The English monarchs also gave more Irish property to English citizens. The Irish became increasingly resentful of England's presence and fought fiercely to retain their land.

James and Ulster

In 1603 the Protestant ruler of Scotland, James, also became king of England. He quickly increased the number of new settlers in Ireland, especially in troublesome and defiant Ulster. He ordered large parcels of Irish land sold or given to English immigrants. In response, the Irish of Ulster killed some of the English who intended to plant themselves in Ireland.

Many Scottish Protestants came to Ireland to settle in the land that James I offered. The newcomers—along with the English troops sent to protect them—built walled towns in which to live.

James continued to deny the Irish their land and the opportunity to follow their own culture. The Irish were not allowed to gather in groups or to work for any of the people who had been planted. Nor could they perform their own music at social gatherings or employ their art forms in building or decoration.

By establishing many more voting districts, James enabled English and Scottish Protestants to win enough seats in the Irish Parliament to easily control the government. The Protestant newcomers used their control of taxes and public works to enrich themselves. By the late 1630s, the 20 percent of the population that had been planted by English kings owned 80 percent of Ireland's land.

Irish Rebellions Continue

In 1641 a group of Irish Catholics attacked the Protestant-led government in Dublin, the leading city of the island. This conflict was the first of a series of clashes in which the Irish evicted many of the king's settlers. English troops tried to contain the Irish rebellions but failed for many years.

Nevertheless, English determination to suppress the Irish grew. In 1649 the English soldier-politician Oliver Cromwell landed near the town of Drogheda with 20,000 troops. In 1652 his army killed thousands of Catholics and defeated several Irish armies. Cromwell took away additional parcels of Irish land.

The English kings Charles II (1660–1685) and James II (1685–1690), who were sympathetic to Catholics, tried to reestablish some rights for the Irish. The Protestant prince William of Orange soon overshadowed these efforts. William challenged James II's right to rule England, Scotland, Wales, and Ireland. In 1690 William's forces defeated James's troops at a battle near the Boyne River in eastern Ireland.

After his victory at the Battle of the Boyne, William became king of Great Britain and Ireland. Many Protestants in Ireland, especially in northern Ireland, had fought on William III's side. Since the eighteenth century, their descendants have gathered in an organization known as the Orange Order to recall the Protestant victory and to strengthen ties among themselves.

By the early 1700s, Irish Catholics held only about 10 percent of the land in Ireland. Most of the territory in the province of Ulster was under Protestant control. During the same period, England, Wales, and Scotland combined to form the United Kingdom of Great Britain (also called Britain). In the north, tensions between Protestants and Catholics increased.

Protestant Leaders

In the 1770s, while Britain was fighting a foreign war to keep its North American colonies, Irish Protestants—mostly from the south—saw an opportunity to gain more independence. Since the British army was busy in North America, few British soldiers remained in Ireland. Irish Protestants established the Irish Volunteers to protect the island from attack by Britain's enemies. Later many Irish-Protestant business leaders demanded broader economic and political freedom from the United Kingdom. These leaders used the Irish Volunteers to help Ireland gain self-rule.

As the British began to lose ground in North America, they found the 40,000 Irish Volunteers too powerful to ignore. Britain agreed to the Protestants' request for a more independent parliament, giving it some authority to make laws.

Photo by Bettmann/Hulton

William of Orange (center on horseback) **and his army defeated the Irish at the Battle of the Boyne in 1690. This English victory strengthened the position of Protestants in the northern part of Ireland. Soon after the battle, William became king of Great Britain and Ireland.**

Certain Protestant leaders from southern Ireland wanted to give Catholics and Protestants the same rights. Theobald Wolfe Tone founded the United Irishmen to pursue this goal. He gathered military support from the French and mounted an attack on British troops in Ireland. The British easily overcame Tone's forces in 1798 and captured Tone as well.

While movements such as Tone's engaged many of the common people of Ireland, not all the Irish supported them. Most Protestant members of Parliament —especially those from Ulster—tried to resist demands for more local, Catholic participation. The Protestants wanted a closer union with Britain and passed legislation in 1800 that transferred control of Ireland directly to the British Parliament.

In 1801 Great Britain and Ireland joined to become the United Kingdom of Great Britain and Ireland. The separate Irish legislature ceased to exist, and Ireland sent its representatives to the British Parliament. Catholics—whether British or Irish—could not be members of Parliament.

Industrialized Ulster

During the nineteenth century, while new industries grew rapidly in Britain, expansion also occurred in northern Ireland. Ulster's shipyards provided many of the vessels that the United Kingdom needed for its worldwide trade. The people in northern Ireland also developed linen-making factories that turned locally grown flax into cloth that could be sold in many markets. Meanwhile, southern Ireland remained primarily a farming region.

British financiers and Irish-Protestant merchants controlled the industries in Ulster. Catholics there had difficulty establishing their own businesses because they did not have the money to begin new enterprises. Many Catholics worked in Protestant-owned factories but usually had low-paying and less secure jobs. Large numbers of rural Catholics moved to Belfast and Londonderry in search of work. Many of these urban immigrants lived in very poor housing and could not find jobs. These inequalities caused tension between Catholics and Protestants.

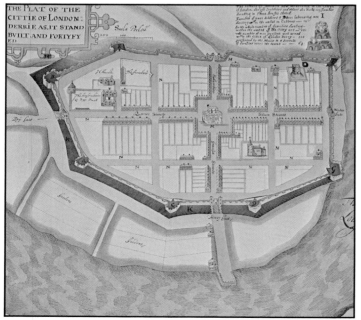

In 1603 the city of Derry in Northern Ireland became known as Londonderry. From 1614 to 1617, the city's Protestant leaders built an 18-foot-thick wall to protect Londonderry from attacks by Irish Catholics. By the 1800s, many Irish of all denominations were coming to the city in search of employment.

In the 1830s, leaders from southern Ireland spoke out for the rights of northern Catholics. In response, the British Parliament passed the Catholic Emancipation Act, which allowed Catholics to seek election to the British legislature. Protestant leaders in northern Ireland, however, changed the voting districts so that Catholics were always in a minority. In this way, it became nearly impossible for Catholics in Ulster to win elections.

In 1845 a blight (a disease caused by a fungus) destroyed that year's crop of potatoes—the staple food for most Irish people. Famine occurred throughout the island. About one million Irish died from starvation or disease during the next several years. The food shortages in Ulster were not as severe as they were in the rest of Ireland. Ulster earned money from its industries and bought food from Britain. The British government did little else to relieve the famine. Thousands of Irish people moved to the United States and other foreign countries to feed their families.

Ulster Opposes Independence

Almost as soon as Ireland began to recover from the potato famine, independence movements gained strength. Both Protestants and Catholics joined groups dedicated to overthrowing British control. In response to pressure from these organizations, the British prime minister—William Gladstone—sponsored new legislation in Parliament. The laws limited the favored status of Protestants and gave Irish-Catholic farmers more rights. Despite these measures, little changed in Ulster.

Protestants there were fearful of separating from Britain. They worried that an independent Ireland would mean financial losses for them, since so much of their trade came from economic cooperation with the United Kingdom. Therefore, the Ulster Protestants worked to maintain close ties with Britain. These people became known as Unionists.

Independent Picture Service

During the Irish potato famine of the late 1840s, many farm families in southern Ireland struggled to find enough to eat. People in the northern parts of the island survived more easily because the region's strong industries made money that funded food purchases from Britain.

On the other side were other Protestants and Catholics who supported independence. They became known as Nationalists because they wanted Ireland to be a separate nation. At the end of the nineteenth century, Arthur Griffith founded Sinn Fein meaning "We Ourselves" as a means of achieving national independence. This organization threatened many of the country's Protestants, especially those in the north whose economic, social, and religious ties were primarily with Britain.

The Early 1900s

The Sinn Fein party and other independence organizations constantly pressured the British Parliament and attempted to shape public opinion. A number of bills proposing independence were put forward in the legislature, but until 1914 none of them

In 1912, when a movement for Irish independence was gaining strength, a large crowd gathered in Belfast to show its support for continued union with Britain.

gained approval. Finally a law was passed that granted the Irish a measure of self-rule.

This bill included Ulster as part of the new country, and the Unionist Protestants quickly opposed the new legislation. Edward Carson of Belfast led the movement against a split with Britain. As a result, another bill was passed in Parliament that excluded Ulster's six predominantly Protestant counties from being part of a new Irish nation. Parliament postponed both laws when World War I broke out in 1914.

About 160,000 Irish Volunteers served alongside the British army during World War I. Sinn Fein members, however, formed the Irish Republican Brotherhood (IRB), a military organization of about 12,000 members, to fight for independence.

Sinn Fein and the IRB led a revolt on the Monday after Easter in 1916. On that day,

about 1,000 rebel fighters seized government buildings in Dublin and proclaimed the independence of the island of Ireland. The Unionist Protestants in the north kept working to supply the British war effort and did not acknowledge the Nationalists' claim.

A British force soon ended the rebellion by Sinn Fein and the IRB. Britain's harsh treatment of rebel prisoners caused public opinion in the south to swing strongly behind the independence movement. As a result, the Sinn Fein party won a majority of the Irish seats in the British Parliament in 1918.

The Sinn Fein members of Parliament formed their own government in 1919 under the leadership of Eamon De Valera and Arthur Griffith. The British sent forces to overcome the new government and the military arm of Sinn Fein—renamed the Irish Republican Army (IRA). Unionists in Ulster formed their own military units and prepared to defend their status as part of Britain. Nationalists and Unionists in Belfast were killed in a series of politically motivated murders from 1920 to 1922.

The Creation of Two Irelands

The British prime minister, David Lloyd George, threatened a full-scale war if Ireland would not submit to British authority. A compromise was reached, and IRA leaders signed a treaty that established the Irish Free State. The new, semi-independent nation had dominion status, meaning that it retained some ties to Britain but was largely self-governing. The 1920 Government of Ireland Act that founded the free state also allowed six of Ulster's counties to remain part of the United Kingdom. This new country was called Northern Ireland.

Southern Ireland became self-governing in 1920. Six counties in the northeast remained part of the United Kingdom as Northern Ireland. In 1921 Unionists, who favored the ties to Britain, won a majority of the seats to the Northern Irish parliament. The Unionist leader, James Craig (above), became the first prime minister of Northern Ireland.

Some IRA members fiercely opposed the establishment of the Irish Free State. The conflict reached Northern Ireland, where several hundred people were killed. Northern Ireland's first prime minister, James Craig, led the Unionist government through these conflicts and through boundary disputes with the Irish Free State. An agreement between Northern Ireland, the Irish Free State, and Britain in 1925 defined the borders between the two parts of Ireland.

Most of the Catholic residents of Northern Ireland did not want the island to be divided. The Protestant people in Ulster, however, did favor division, or partition, if it helped to maintain ties with Britain. To make sure their point of view would win, Protestant political leaders drew the boundaries of voting districts so that none would have a Catholic majority. Also, some people—Protestant business leaders, for example—were allowed to vote as many as six times in local elections.

Elected councils, which influenced housing and employment decisions, often neglected the needs of the Catholic people in their districts. For these reasons, Catholics became even more cut off from the Protestant majority in Northern Ireland. Meanwhile, in southern Ireland, the Irish Free State proclaimed its complete independence in 1936 and changed its name to the Republic of Ireland in 1949.

North-South Relations

Tensions increased in Northern Ireland between 1925 and 1945. The IRA in the south sent soldiers across the border into Northern Ireland to attack the Royal Ulster Constabulary (RUC)—the official police force of Northern Ireland. The IRA also fired upon British soldiers who were sent to protect the population of Northern Ireland.

The RUC and the British forces were strengthened by the Ulster Special Constabulary—also known as the B-Specials

—a group of all-Protestant volunteers. The government of Northern Ireland wrote the Special Powers Act in 1922 to give the police and the military more authority. The new powers included rights to search without warrants and to hold prisoners without charging them with a crime. The Special Powers Act allowed local authorities to prevent newspapers from being published. It also stopped people from bringing legal cases against the government.

The police forces used these laws to control the rebellious Catholic population of Northern Ireland and to keep the IRA from crossing the southern border. Catholic anti-partition groups often held parades in the early 1930s to promote their cause. But the Special Powers Act soon prohibited these gatherings. In 1935 resentful Catholics started several riots after the Protestant Orange Order was allowed to hold its annual parade.

Northern Ireland was not Europe's only scene of conflict. In the late 1930s, Germany expanded its territory, a move that threatened other European nations, including Britain. World War II broke out in 1939. During the conflict, Northern Ireland contributed to the British war effort through shipbuilding and textile manufacturing. Britain positioned troops in Northern Ireland, which made the area a target for German military planes. As a result, Belfast was heavily bombed.

Protestants easily kept Catholics out of power in Northern Ireland during the war years. After the war ended in 1945, anti-partition feeling swelled when the Irish Free State became the Republic of Ireland. Protestant Unionists remained in control of the north, and the British Parliament

The Orange Order, a Protestant organization, has many branches throughout Northern Ireland. Each club holds annual parades in which members wear uniforms that indicate the name of their neighborhood or town.

reaffirmed Northern Ireland's status as part of the United Kingdom.

In 1956 the IRA began another series of attacks on Northern Ireland. Its members planted bombs in public places, targeting British soldiers and RUC forces. The IRA also set ambushes for trucks that carried government supplies or personnel. The campaign against northern targets started with a burst of activity but trailed off over a period of years. The level of violence offended many people and won the IRA little support. At this time, most Catholics in Northern Ireland and in the Republic did not support the IRA. By 1962 the IRA offensive was over.

Movement for Civil Rights

In 1963 Terence O'Neill was elected prime minister of Northern Ireland. A leader of the Unionist party, O'Neill nevertheless wanted to bridge the gulf between Protes-

Photo by Bettmann/Hulton

Ian Paisley led the movement to prevent agreement between the Unionists and Nationalists. Here, two policemen escort him away from a demonstration.

Independent Picture Service

In the 1960s, Northern Ireland's prime minister Terence O'Neill tried without success to bridge the gap between his Unionist party and the Nationalist party. The Nationalists wanted to join Northern Ireland with the Republic of Ireland to form one nation.

tants and Catholics. O'Neill's government funded new industries, built new public housing, and repaired the country's roads, bridges, and harbors. O'Neill also held meetings with the prime minister of the Republic to smooth relations between the two parts of Ireland.

In 1966 Ian Paisley, a minister of the Protestant Free Presbyterian Church, started a movement to block O'Neill's efforts to bring Catholics and Protestants closer together. Paisley's speeches heightened anti-Catholic sentiments among some Protestants. His supporters marched in parades sponsored by the Orange Order, which created a tense public atmosphere.

The Ulster Volunteer Force (UVF), a Unionist military organization, attracted many backers in the mid-1960s. The UVF searched out IRA members still in Northern Ireland and murdered them. The activities of Paisley and the UVF on one side and the increasing demands of the Catholic minority on the other side made O'Neill's task very difficult.

Members of the Royal Ulster Constabulary—the official police force in Northern Ireland—had to dodge rocks during a riot in Belfast in 1969.

In 1967 a civil rights movement started in Northern Ireland, when Catholic activists founded the Northern Ireland Civil Rights Association (NICRA) in Belfast. NICRA members wanted to achieve fair access to housing, to job opportunities, and to political representation. Most new housing, for example, went to Protestant citizens, even in districts that were mostly Catholic in population. The Catholics also sought to overturn the laws that allowed searches and seizures of their property without a court order.

The civil rights workers organized protest marches, which the Unionists answered with counter-marches. In this way, each group hoped to strengthen its own influence and to weaken the support of the other side. The tension between the two groups eventually centered on the Catholic neighborhood of Bogside in Londonderry, which became an urban battlefield. Across hastily built barricades, Catholics and Protestants threw rocks and gasoline bombs at one another. Sniping was common, putting Bogsiders against police, soldiers, and Protestant Unionists.

Amid this growing conflict, Catholic voters in central Ulster elected Bernadette Devlin, a civil rights activist, to the British Parliament in 1969. Devlin's speeches before Parliament and in Northern Ireland swayed British public opinion to support the Catholics' fight for fair treatment. Her

In 1970 Bernadette Devlin, who represented Northern Ireland in the British Parliament, was convicted of causing a riot in Belfast.

pleas for change in the structure of Northern Ireland's government could not, however, stem the violence.

Divisions Deepen

As the violence increased, the IRA became active again. It viewed the escalating conflict as a chance to achieve a united, independent Ireland. A wing of the IRA began training soldiers to carry out terrorist activities in Northern Ireland.

A march by the Orange Order in 1970 provided the first occasion for an IRA attack. Protestants and Catholics of Belfast turned the Orange Order's march into a rock-throwing battle. The British army tried unsuccessfully to separate the two groups, and seven bystanders were killed.

Later IRA actions included bombings of Protestant businesses and sniping during confrontations between British troops and Catholic rioters. In response, British troops changed their tactics. Instead of trying to ease difficult situations, the troops confronted Catholic protesters. As a result, Catholics viewed the IRA as a protector and supported it.

Courtesy of David Gibson

Courtesy of David Gibson

Wall paintings and graffiti appear throughout urban areas of Northern Ireland. Both the Unionists *(above)*, who remember the victories of the past, and the Nationalists *(left)*, who condemn the injustices of the present, use these art forms to express their beliefs.

35

Photo by Belfast Telegraph

In 1971 stone-throwing protestors and British army troops confronted each other in Londonderry's Catholic neighborhood of Bogside.

In 1971 British and Northern Irish leaders answered these acts by adopting a policy of internment without trial, meaning that people suspected of being terrorists could be arrested and held indefinitely. At the beginning of the internment program, the British army made a sweep of Catholic strongholds and arrested about 350 people. This action deeply outraged Northern Ireland's Catholics, and IRA activity increased. At the same time, Protestant groups began to engage in their own terrorist activities.

Recent Events

The British government banned all marches in Northern Ireland in August 1971. Nevertheless, Catholic civil rights activists felt that marching was one of the best ways to nonviolently express their views. In January 1972, the Catholic activists organized a march of 6,000 people through Londonderry. British soldiers were on hand to keep order. People from the edge of the crowd began to throw rocks at the British soldiers, who arrested the attackers. The crowd panicked, shots were fired, and 13 marchers were killed. In the two weeks after this event, more than 300 terrorist acts occurred.

As a result of the increased violence, Britain suspended the Northern Irish government in March 1972. British authorities named a secretary of state for Northern Ireland who would administer the country directly for Britain. Catholic-Protestant terrorism continued alongside nonviolent civil rights actions and peace efforts. In 1976 two Belfast women—Mairead Corrigan and Betty Williams—won the Nobel Peace Prize for their work to halt the fighting between Catholics and Protestants.

In 1985 Britain—on behalf of Northern Ireland—and the Republic of Ireland entered into the Anglo-Irish Agreement to promote stability in Northern Ireland. One of the agreement's main sections stated that a change in Northern Ireland's status

These young members of the Orange Order branch, the Sons of William *(left),* participate in a Protestant parade. Meanwhile, Roman Catholic children *(below)* learn from graffiti the strong views held by Catholics in Northern Ireland.

Photo © Rachel Giese

Photo © Rachel Giese

would occur only by a majority vote of the Northern Irish people. Another provision established official lines of communication between Northern Ireland and the Republic of Ireland so that the two countries would discuss affairs of mutual interest.

In the 1990s, the Irish, British, and Northern Irish governments tried on a number of occasions to settle Northern Ireland's political future. Their efforts were repeatedly set back by acts of terrorism or strong disagreements over the terms of negotiation. Whether Northern Ireland will achieve a lasting peace remains unclear.

Government

The United Kingdom of Great Britain and Northern Ireland has no written constitution. Instead, various parliamentary acts and common laws form the basis of government. Although symbolically headed by a monarch, the nation is governed by Parliament.

Parliament enacted the Government of Ireland Act of 1920 to establish a separate parliament for Northern Ireland. Since 1972, however, this parliament has been suspended. Under its charter, 52 delegates serve in Northern Ireland's House of Commons for terms that last no more than five years. The House selects the 24 members of the Senate, who serve terms of eight years. House members also choose Northern Ireland's prime minister from the political party that controls the most seats.

Since the suspension, a secretary of state for Northern Ireland has administered the country and reports on its status to the British Parliament each year. Usually, this officer stresses the necessity of continuing the governmental suspension.

Northern Ireland relies on Parliament for legislation on defense, foreign policy, and international trade. Northern Ireland elects 17 parliamentary members to this national legislative body.

Northern Ireland's judicial system is similar to those used in England and Wales. Courts make decisions based on parliamentary legislation and common law. The most serious criminal offenses are tried by the Crown Court, which usually consists of a judge and a jury. Magistrate courts hear less serious cases. Appeals are made to either the appropriate county court or to the Northern Ireland Court of Appeals. A final judicial appeal can be made to the nine-judge court in the British House of Lords.

Northern Ireland has 26 districts, each of which has an elected council. Belfast and Londonderry have their own councils, and 12 other regional councils exist. They focus on public works, education, public health, and local planning.

Photo © Rachel Giese

By covering up the reference to London, a protester expresses anti-British feeling. The roadside marker reflects the ongoing divisions that exist within Northern Ireland.

These children attend school in County Antrim. **More money is spent on education in Northern Ireland than in England, Wales, and Scotland**—the other countries within the United Kingdom.

3) The People

Of the 59 million inhabitants of the United Kingdom, about 1.6 million live in Northern Ireland. More than half of the population resides in Belfast and its suburbs and in Londonderry. The eastern coast is the most densely settled area in Northern Ireland. In the western half of the country, small towns occasionally break an almost completely rural landscape.

Ethnic and Religious Identity

About half of Northern Ireland's population are descendants of Scottish and English settlers. These Northern Irish follow the Protestant religion and have strong ties to the United Kingdom.

Nearly 40 percent of the country's citizens are Roman Catholics, who have ancestral links to the earlier Celtic, Viking, and Norman inhabitants of Ireland. The Catholic population, historically the minority, is growing faster than the Protestant population.

Since the 1600s, when most of the Scots and the English first came to Northern Ireland, little intermarrying has occurred between new arrivals and the original Irish population. An age-old separation based on religious, ethnic, and economic grounds continues to the present day.

Efforts to overcome this major ethnic division have not been very successful. Generally, both groups disapprove of schools that mix Protestants and Catholics. Government housing projects keep Catholic and Protestant populations largely separated. Proposals for new economic developments almost always are based on ethnic loyalties. Nevertheless, individuals on both sides of the conflict continue to work toward positive contact between the two groups.

Sensitivity to religious membership is very high in Northern Ireland. While Roman Catholics belong to a single religious group, the people of the Protestant majority belong to several different sects. The largest is the Presbyterian Church, followed by the Church of Ireland and the Methodist Church.

The largest Protestant organization is the Orange Order, a group founded in northeastern Ireland in 1795. In the early 1990s, the order had about 90,000 members. The order draws its support from several different Protestant religious groups and works to improve the position of the country's Protestant citizens. To publicly display its strength, the order holds an annual parade on July 12 to celebrate the victory of Prince William of Orange over King James II at the Battle of the Boyne in 1690.

In hopes of overcoming inequalities in job opportunities, in way of life, and in other matters, many Catholic clergy participate in the country's civil rights movement. When civil rights activists march through the streets of Northern Ireland, they often carry banners and artworks that are part of the Catholic religion. Many illustrations that are painted on the sides of buildings have a religious message as well.

Holidays and political rallies with religious overtones allow Northern Irish Catholics to express their loyalties. Having experienced harsh treatment by the Protestant majority, many Catholics hope that Northern Ireland will one day unite with the Republic of Ireland.

Photo by UPI/Bettmann Newsphotos

Catholics and Protestants who called themselves "Peace People" joined together at this 1976 rally in London. They were led by Betty Williams *(wearing dark glasses)* who won the Nobel Peace Prize for her efforts to stop the fighting in Northern Ireland.

Cardinal John O'Connor of New York speaks to Catholics at St. Patrick's Cathedral in Armagh. One-third of Northern Ireland's citizens are Roman Catholic.

Many Protestants belong to the Orange Order, which was organized to celebrate the victory of William of Orange over James II at the Battle of the Boyne. Orangemen march in parades accompanied by the beat of huge Lambeg drums.

Catholic neighborhoods in Northern Ireland's cities consist mainly of small row houses. Residents sometimes paint graffiti on fences and on the sides of dwellings to express political views.

Photo © Rachel Giese

Way of Life

Northern Irish Catholics and Northern Irish Protestants lead very different lifestyles. Most of the country's business leaders have traditionally come from the Protestant majority. Throughout the region's history, Protestants have given well-paying jobs to other Protestants. As a result, most Catholic workers are poorer than Protestant laborers are. Many Protestant citizens of Northern Ireland are also struggling to find economic success, although fewer Protestants than Catholics are unemployed.

For years, Catholic residents of Belfast and Londonderry have lived in narrow row houses, which share a common wall with the dwellings on either side. The fronts of

Photo © Rachel Giese

Some rural Catholic families live in stone or brick cottages. Built in the nineteenth century, many of these homes are deteriorating.

these buildings are often close to the street. It is not uncommon for toilets to be in the backyard, unattached to the house. The government has funded many housing projects throughout Northern Ireland. Until recently, however, Protestant officials—who controlled the distribution of these new apartments and houses —gave them only to other Protestants.

Catholics make up a large percentage of Northern Ireland's rural population. Some of these families live in nineteenth-century houses, which have stone or brick walls and sometimes are covered by thatched roofs. One common method of heating rural homes is by burning dried peat.

Communities of all sizes have "pubs"— an abbreviation for public houses. At these

As members of the United Kingdom, Northern Irish children get the benefit of the National Health Service—a kingdom-wide health-care system. This readily available and low-cost medical care is largely responsible for the country's positive health statistics, a measure of the quality of life in Northern Ireland.

places, residents of a neighborhood often go to visit with one another, to drink refreshments, and sometimes to have a meal. Earlier in the twentieth century, many pubs served a largely male clientele, but in recent decades women have become regular patrons as well.

For much of the twentieth century, the role of women in Northern Ireland has been that of the traditional homemaker. This way of life began to change for Northern Irish women in the 1980s, when many joined the business and industrial work force. In the early 1990s, through the enforcement of new laws, women were overcoming discrimination in hiring practices and in unequal pay. The Equal Opportunities Commission of Northern Ireland monitors businesses to make sure the laws are followed.

Education

Northern Ireland spends more money on education per student than do the other countries within the United Kingdom. More than 95 percent of the Northern Irish people can read and write. Children between the ages of 5 and 16 are required to attend school.

For the most part, elementary students who are Catholic attend private Catholic schools, where teachers instruct them in the Gaelic language as well as in English. Most elementary students who are Protestant go to state-run schools, where they receive instruction only in English. Very few schools enroll both Catholic and Protestant students.

Secondary education, which students finish at 16, offers a wide variety of subjects for study. About 65 percent of secondary-school graduates continue their education. Some choose vocational or technical training. Others prepare to enter a university when they reach the age of 18.

Queen's University in Belfast was founded in 1845 and enrolls about 7,000 students. In 1968 the New University of Ulster opened in the town of Coleraine, and this institution now has a student body of about 2,000. Technical schools include the Belfast College of Technology founded in 1901 and Ulster Polytechnic, which was established in the town of Newtownabbey in 1978.

Courtesy of David Gibson

Most schools in Northern Ireland are segregated by religion. Many Catholic students go to private schools that are operated by a local Roman Catholic church. Most Protestant students attend state-run schools that do not have religious ties.

Dressed as a shoemaker, a rhymer in Armagh threads an imaginary needle for a fascinated audience. Rhymers are poets and storytellers who perform in both Gaelic and English for schoolchildren throughout Northern Ireland.

The Arts

The Northern Irish have inherited Celtic artistic traditions from both Irish and Scottish people. Their age-old musical instruments include fiddles, bagpipes, drums, flutes, and harps. Folk music is frequently performed in pubs, where people come to socialize over food and drink. Music almost always accompanies parades and religious services. Classical music also has a strong following in Northern Ireland. The Ulster National Orchestra and the Philharmonic Society have their headquarters in Belfast and play concerts throughout the country.

Northern Ireland is the birthplace of several twentieth-century authors. C. Day Lewis (1904–1972) taught and translated classical literature, as well as wrote novels and verse. He was named poet laureate of the United Kingdom in 1970. Louis MacNeice was born in Belfast but lived in England most of his life. He also taught classical literature in British colleges and wrote and produced radio shows. His poetry often uses Celtic imagery. Seamus Heaney (born in 1939) was brought up on a farm in Northern Ireland. He attended Queen's University and later wrote poetry for the Belfast magazine *Phoenix*.

Bright colors and intricate patterns are trademarks of Northern Ireland's fine linens. Although most linen is now produced in factories, many craftspeople still make the cloth by hand.

Health and Social Welfare

As part of the United Kingdom, Northern Ireland participates in the National Health Service that the central government started in the 1950s. The Department of Health and Social Services in Northern Ireland administers the health-care system locally. Many services, such as maternity care and hospitalization, are free, while dental treatment and some types of medical care are provided at a charge. Taxes support these national health programs.

Health statistics in Northern Ireland are favorable when compared with those of the rest of Europe. The infant mortality rate is 6.1 deaths per 1,000 live births, compared to 11 per 1,000 for Europe as a whole. The average life expectancy for the Northern Irish is 76 years. Among the most common illnesses in the country are heart disease and cancer.

Northern Ireland also participates in national social-welfare programs to help people maintain a basic standard of living. For example, social-security funds support many widowed, elderly, ill, unemployed, and disabled citizens. Periods of high unemployment, when many people collect welfare money, put pressure on local and national budgets of both Northern Ireland and the United Kingdom.

Food

People in Northern Ireland have fairly simple diets. Breakfast may consist of bacon, eggs, mushrooms, and tomatoes. Porridge (hot oatmeal) also is often eaten at the start of the day. In the middle of the morning, the Northern Irish stop for a cup of tea or coffee with cookies or farls—hollow buttermilk biscuits.

This bakery in Northern Ireland offers a variety of breads. Whole-meal brown bread and plain white soda bread are served regularly with meals and snacks.

Most households share the main meal at midday. Entrees may feature beef, chicken, pork, lamb, or fish—usually trout, plaice, lobster, salmon, or scallops. Potatoes are a common Northern Irish vegetable, as are onions, cabbage, peas, and carrots. Cooks of Northern Ireland are known for making many varieties of bread.

Dessert—puddings or baked pastries— or cheese complete the main meal or can be eaten at other times of the day. The Irish often break for tea or other refreshment during the afternoon. The final daily meal may be as simple as toast and eggs or might be made up of leftovers from earlier meals.

Urban restaurants *(right and below)* take advantage of the fruits, vegetables, and other foods that can be grown in Northern Ireland's rich soil. Diners have also come to enjoy the many varieties of fish that are caught and served daily.

Courtesy of Northern Ireland Tourist Board

Courtesy of Northern Ireland Tourist Board

Northern Ireland's clear rivers and lakes hold an abundance of fresh-water fish, making angling a popular sport for visitors and local folk.

Courtesy of Northern Ireland Tourist Board

Sports and Recreation

Sports played in other parts of the British Isles are also popular in Northern Ireland. The country has more than 500 amateur teams dedicated to soccer, which is called football in Europe. Semiprofessional teams play in competitions throughout Ireland and Britain, as well as in tournaments in other nations. Fewer people play rugby (a rough field sport similar to U.S. football),

Courtesy of Northern Ireland Tourist Board

Lough Erne, with its sparkling waters and steady breezes, is a favorite spot for sailing.

49

but many enjoy watching it. Invented in England during the sixteenth century, cricket is a popular ball-and-bat game that pits two teams of 11 players against each other.

Golfers play on fine courses throughout Northern Ireland, especially along the eastern coast of the country. Courses near Portrush and Newcastle have hosted major tournaments. Freshwater and deep-sea fishing attract many enthusiasts. Brown trout run in several of Lough Neagh's inflowing rivers, including the Lower Bann, the Blackwater, and the Moyola. Sea trout return from ocean waters to breed in the rivers in July and August, providing good sport for fly-fishing.

Many Northern Irish enjoy horse and dog races and bet on the results. The horse track at Downpatrick is among the most famous in the country. Horse shows are commonly held from February to October. Walking, particularly along the Antrim coast and through the Mourne Mountains, is a favorite pastime for visitors and residents alike. Billiards, chess, and darts are popular indoor activities that people often play in pubs.

Courtesy of Northern Ireland Tourist Board

Golfers putt on a green at the Royal Portrush Golf Club, one of more than 70 golf courses throughout Northern Ireland.

Courtesy of Northern Ireland Tourist Board

The races at Downpatrick have an enthusiastic following. Bookmaking – a system of betting – is legal in Northern Ireland, and bookmakers set odds and accept wagers for each race.

Photo © Rachel Giese

During a rugby game, players may make a scrum – a formation that links some players into a tunnel-like group. The ball is then tossed into the center, and players try to kick it to a teammate outside the scrum.

Northern Ireland is famous for its fine-quality textiles. This Jacquard loom, named after its eighteenth-century French inventor, weaves intricately patterned cloth.

Independent Picture Service

4) The Economy

Northern Ireland was the first region of Ireland to develop large industries. The English and Scottish immigrants to the area maintained ties with their homelands, and these links eventually brought trade benefits. In the 1990s, Northern Ireland still did more business across the sea with the United Kingdom than it did with the Republic of Ireland to the south.

The traditionally strong industries of shipbuilding and linen manufacturing continued to decline through the early 1990s. As a result, the rate of unemployment for Northern Irish workers rose very high—sometimes reaching nearly 20 percent of the work force. The national government offered tax advantages and other business incentives to local and overseas investors

Workers at a U.S.-owned tool company in Northern Ireland manufacture oil-well drill bits. To curb the country's high unemployment rate, the Northern Irish government tries hard to attract foreign businesses with tax breaks and other incentives.

to encourage them to develop new businesses in Northern Ireland.

Manufacturing and Trade

Northern Ireland has long been recognized as a center of textile and clothing manufacturing. Locally grown flax plants once provided the fibers to make linen, but in recent decades most of the flax has been imported. Woolen materials, cotton fabrics, and artificial fibers have replaced linen as the mainstays of the country's textile industry. Most of these products are made in Belfast. Clothing manufacturing, especially of shirts and pajamas, is centered in Londonderry.

Many mills in Northern Ireland manufacture cord, twine, and rope. Here, laborers attach empty spools to machines that quickly wind the rope.

Shipbuilding is one of Belfast's key industries. In fact, Belfast has the largest shipyard in the United Kingdom. The same engineering and construction skills that are used to assemble large oceangoing vessels have also been put to use in airplane manufacturing. Northern Ireland also has some factories that make auto parts.

Many of the foods produced in rural Northern Ireland—especially dairy products, meat, and potatoes—are brought to Belfast to be packed for shipment or prepared for sale. Belfast workers also make fine liquors that are sold throughout the world.

About 18 percent of employed Northern Irish work in the manufacturing sector of the economy. About one-half of the goods that the country exports go to England, Wales, and Scotland. Likewise, most of the imports needed for industrial production—minerals, oil, machinery, and raw materials, for example—come from the United Kingdom.

Courtesy of Harland & Wolff

Northern Ireland has the largest shipyard in the United Kingdom. Since the early 1800s, this facility in Belfast has built warships and ocean liners, including the famous *Titanic*, which sank in 1912 during its first voyage.

Cone-shaped piles of hay stand ready to be bundled. Some of the hay planted in Northern Ireland provides feed for animals.

Sweeping expanses of pastureland for cattle and sheep cover much of the country. In many cases, landowners have combined small farms into large, productive estates.

Agriculture and Fishing

About 10.5 percent of the Northern Irish work force is employed in agriculture. This percentage is three times as high as the rate in the rest of the United Kingdom. Farms have typically been small throughout the country's history. In recent decades, however, the number of farms has declined as small acreages have been combined to create larger farms. More farms now have tractors and other machinery, which help to make agricultural work more efficient and profitable.

Most of the farmland is used as pasture for livestock. About 85 percent of Northern Ireland's agricultural income comes from raising cattle, sheep, pigs, and chickens. To keep the soil fertile, crops such as oats and potatoes are planted in fields only after they have been used as grassland for several years. Apple and pear orchards exist south of Lough Neagh. Other Northern Irish agricultural products include turnips, barley, and hay.

55

Farmers rotate crops, such as oats and barley, with grassland to keep the soil fertile and full of healthy nutrients. Crop rotation dates from the 1700s and allows farmers to produce crops on all their land throughout the year.

Bidders at an auction in Ballymena, in central County Antrim, study a well-fattened pig before shouting their offers.

Independent Picture Service

Tourism is a growing economic activity in Northern Ireland. Many travelers enjoy the country's natural beauty, including rolling hills, low mountains, and rural lanes.

Northern Ireland has both saltwater and freshwater fishing grounds. Fishermen haul in their saltwater catches off the eastern coast, netting scallops, whiting, and herring. Throughout Lough Erne, Lough Neagh, and other lakes, the main varieties of fish are salmon, trout, and eel from local fisheries.

Tourism and Transportation

Receiving 1.5 million visitors per year, Northern Ireland has a significant tourist trade—especially considering the civil unrest that plagues the country. The landscape and natural beauty draw many vacationers, and other travelers are attracted by a desire to visit the land of their ancestors. The national tourist authorities recognize that tourism will not grow significantly until tensions and political violence within the country lessen.

The scenery of the Mourne Mountains attracts many visitors. In County Fermanagh, the town of Enniskillen sits at the juncture of Upper and Lower Lough Erne.

Courtesy of Northern Ireland Tourist Board

An Irish aristocrat built the Mussenden Temple on his estate in Downhill in 1783. A memorial and library, the building attracts many tourists.

On a clear day, Garron Point in County Antrim offers hikers a view of Scotland across the North Channel.

Visitors to the Armagh Observatory enjoy models of spacecraft, video shows of the sky, and hands-on computer displays.

Crowds cheer as participants in a tug-of-war drag their opponents through the mud. Local festivals in Northern Ireland entertain residents and foreigners alike.

Once the home of many ancient Irish chiefs, Enniskillen is a hub of tourist activity in the region. County Antrim along the northeastern coast also has beautiful rolling hills, headlands that jut out into the ocean, and many picturesque towns.

A number of festivals and sporting events bring people to Northern Ireland throughout the year. Belfast Festival, held annually at Queen's University in November, mixes performances of classical, jazz, and folk music with dance and film events.

A brass band performs in Bangor, a seaside resort near Belfast. The capital also offers tourists opportunities to hear classical and traditional music.

59

Ferries transport passengers and cars between Northern Ireland and Great Britain. This vessel travels between Stranraer in Scotland and Larne in County Antrim.

Courtesy of Northern Ireland Tourist Board

People can bus to almost any destination in Northern Ireland. The Ulsterbus Company operates all overland services on the country's extensive network of roads.

Courtesy of David Gibson

Ould Lammas Fair occurs in Londonderry each November. The town of Downpatrick hosts a famous horse race, the Ulster Harp National, in February. In May many people come to participate in or watch the Ulster Games, an international sporting competition.

Northern Ireland has a well-developed transportation network that connects cities, towns, and small villages. Often the roads are narrow, but they are well-maintained. About 200 miles of railway serve the population, linking the large urban centers. A few inland waterways carry commercial and pleasure boats. A sea channel on the Upper Bann River leads to Coleraine, for example.

Boats and planes link Northern Ireland to Great Britain. Many residents depend on high-speed transportation to conduct business, as well as to maintain family ties. Belfast is the country's major port, followed in importance by Londonderry, Larne, and Coleraine. Several ports send ferries to Scotland and England. For instance, the Belfast ferries travel to Glasgow in west central Scotland and to Liverpool in western England. Airlines using Belfast International Airport provide service to many cities throughout the world.

Energy and Mining

Most of Northern Ireland's energy is imported. Farm families, as well as some companies, however, favor locally produced peat as a low-cost fuel. People cut peat by hand with sharp blades, shaping the material into small blocks that are stacked on end to dry. The blocks are then taken to homes to be burned like wood. Companies that harvest peat on a large scale use machines for cutting and gathering.

Northern Ireland has few minerals, and those that exist are not abundant enough to support extensive mining operations. Nevertheless, several thousand workers extract the country's basalt, limestone, granite, sand, and gravel. These materials are used to construct roads and buildings.

A worker uses a long-handled tool to cut into a layer of peat, which is a major domestic fuel in Northern Ireland. The first stage of coal, peat is formed when partly decayed plants are pressed into layers in swamps and marshes over a very long period. The layers range in color from a yellowish brown on top to dark brown at the bottom, where the peat is very soggy. Harvesters cut the peat into blocks, which are then dried and burned. Factories use peat to stoke generators that make electricity. In rural areas, residents burn the blocks to heat their homes, stacking the peat next to their cottages for use throughout the year.

The Future

By the early 1990s, Northern Ireland's leaders had reduced some of the long-standing inequalities between Catholics and Protestants. As a result of governmental efforts, better housing and increased job opportunities were available on a fairer basis to members of both religious groups. According to many Northern Irish, improvements in the country's economic health will reduce conflicts between Protestants and Catholics.

The main political factions—the Unionists and the Nationalists—are far from agreeing on how to share power. They are also divided about what Northern Ireland's relationship to the Republic of Ireland should be. Neither side can figure

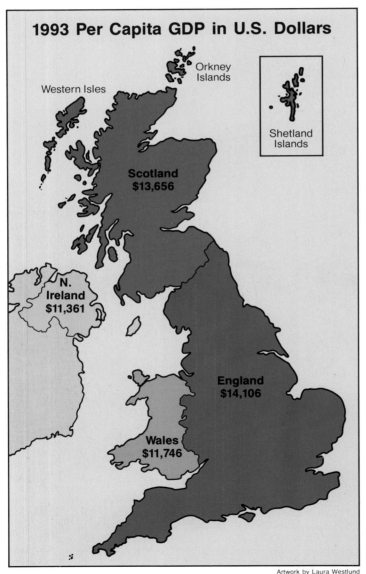

1993 Per Capita GDP in U.S. Dollars

Orkney Islands

Western Isles

Shetland Islands

Scotland $13,656

N. Ireland $11,361

England $14,106

Wales $11,746

Artwork by Laura Westlund

This map compares the average wealth per person—calculated by gross domestic product (GDP) per capita—for the four countries that make up the United Kingdom. The GDP is the value of all goods and services produced within the borders of each country in a year. To arrive at the GDP per capita, each country's total GDP is divided by its population. The resulting dollar amounts indicate one measure of the quality of life in the countries of the United Kingdom. The overall GDP figure for the United Kingdom is $13,872. Northern Ireland's figure—the lowest in the kingdom—reflects the country's recent economic difficulties. The Northern Irish government has worked hard to reduce the high unemployment rate by trying to attract new businesses. The country's history of political conflict and violence has hindered these efforts. As part of the United Kingdom, however, Northern Ireland's people qualify for medical and social-welfare benefits that enable them to maintain a good standard of living. (Data taken from *Britain 1996*, prepared by the Central Office of Information.)

On July 12, Protestants throughout Northern Ireland celebrate the anniversary of the Battle of the Boyne by marching in parades. The people decorate drums with blossoms of orange lilies and sweet william, which are symbols of Protestant patriotism.

out what role, if any, the United Kingdom will play in Northern Ireland's government. Factions within these two groups continue to block decisions that might lead to solutions. Until Protestants and Catholics can find more common ground, Northern Ireland's future will remain troubled and uncertain.

Catholics participate in the annual Easter parade in Londonderry. Promoting national independence, their banner reads Sinn Fein, meaning "We Ourselves." Sinn Fein, a political party, seeks to end Northern Ireland's ties to the United Kingdom.

Index